CELEBRATING THE SOUL CYCLE

Meditations on the Four Seasons

By Britta Kantzer

MN
P

Magic Note Press

ISBN: 978-0-615-27841-4

Published by Magic Note Press
Campbell, California
www.magicnotepress.com

DEDICATION

This book is dedicated to those men and women who know that man's real purpose in life is to manifest the one guiding cosmic principle on Earth: it existed before time and is the realization of Unity, the spiritualization of the Earth through love.

CONTENTS

FOREWORD

I am flattered to have been invited to contribute a Foreword to this beautiful book.

When I was setting up the Ardue Web site as a contribution to holistic adult education, I felt a need to provide readers with something more than mere reading matter — some means by which those who felt so inclined might actively participate with myself and each other to constitute a kind of "cyber-community".

The first part of the Ardue project therefore took the form of a Temple – a place set aside for meditation and contemplation. In such a context, it seemed natural to introduce a form of ritual which readers could re-enact in their own homes. My sense of personal inadequacy to design such a ritual prompted me to seek assistance through the medium of a mailing list of which I happened to be a member. Britta Kantzer generously offered to help. She not only designed four imaginative forms of ritual for celebration of the Solstices and Equinoxes, but also contributed appropriate discourses to be read aloud by the participant in the ritual.

The twelve essays which constitute this book originated as ritual discourses for the Ardue Temple. It gives me great joy to reflect that I was privileged to act as midwife at their birth.

Britta and I have never met face to face, but her practical help and deeply spiritual discourses have been a great comfort and inspiration for me. It is a delight to see her profound thoughts so beautifully presented in print.

Duncan Macdonald

When Life to Joy Awakens

"There are only two ways to live your life. One is as though nothing is a miracle. The other is as though everything is a miracle".

— Albert Einstein

My New Year's resolutions began with the acquisition of a new calendar — but not a regular German calendar. It had to be in French, which would help me to practise and improve my language skills while serving as a calendar too. One morning, while ripping off a new page ready for another French lesson, I noticed that there were tiny icons and numbers at the bottom of the paper. They gave the exact time of sunrise and sunset for the day.

I think I had concentrated so much on the new French words that the icons of the Sun and Moon and the numbers had not previously caught my attention. I stared at them as if I had never seen them before. Curiously I turned to the following pages, and was surprised to see with what regularity the Sun rises a little earlier each day and sets a little later. How often had I myself referred to "the days getting longer" without realizing the orderliness of the daily progression of the Sun on its course through the year. Now it seemed as if, with this calendar, I had found a new entry to understanding the mysterious rhythm of the solar cycle in which the Earth makes one complete circuit around the Sun. What does the relationship between Sun and Earth and their respective energies mean for us?

Aren't we also made of the same energies and sustained by them? Isn't our body built up of a spectrum of vibrating energies? Clairvoyant people and mystics of all ages have described these energies as different levels and bodies and taught that our identification with a physical body defines our three-dimensional reality. But there are higher realities much more wondrous than the one to which we are accustomed. Expanding the consciousness means raising our awareness of these vibrations and so enabling us to contact these higher vibrational worlds.

We must make an effort to imprint into our minds that our bodies, like the rest of creation, are ever-changing dynamic fields of energy, and that this mysterious energy, sometimes called the creative Universal Life-Force, is spiritual energy and manifests two-fold: as active, outgoing, positive force and as passive, receptive, negative force. From the interchange and play of these forces all forms are created.

From quantum physics we know that matter and energy are interchangeable. It validates what mystics have always said — that matter is condensed spirit energy and that spirit is the fundamental generator of matter. Thus we can view our bodies as manifestations of spirit energy. This spirit-body-continuum can be understood adequately only when we appreciate ourselves as an ever-changing energy system that interacts continuously with the energy surrounding us. We respond to this dance of energies mostly unconsciously. The old adage, "Know your Self and you will know God and the Universe", suddenly rings true when we realise that everything which manifests as substance and force is composed of the same energy.

How does the seasonal flow of energy influence our own energy-field? How do we respond to the waxing and waning of solar energy? What role do the equinoxes and solstices play? Are they significant times in the annual cycle to which we can adapt positively?

When the whole Universe can be defined as one infinite universal energy-field with different degrees of lower and higher vibrational forms, we can no longer legitimately separate matter from spirit, the visible from the invisible. There is no abstract spirit on one side and nature devoid of spirit on the other, but nature permeated with creative spirit energy naturally forming and shaping all into one-ness. From this we can deduce that we are always connected, bathed in this flow of energy within and around us. Nature is singing the great song of creation, responding instinctively to the driving rhythmic power of the creative cosmic life force. In India this is known as "Shiva's drum", the heartbeat of the Universe.

If we attune to the rhythm of this flow, we benefit in our harmonious development and simultaneously convey impulses of beneficial energy to our immediate environment. The rhythm of this inbreathing and out breathing of energy defines the annual and daily cycles and stages of all life. Out of winter comes spring, spring turns into summer, summer gives way to autumn, autumn shades into winter, and another round begins. This is the great dance of energy between Sun and Earth, whereby the Sun may be regarded as the positive and active pole and the Earth as the negative and passive pole. Both are equal partners in this cosmic dance. Their interchanging, harmoniously blending contributions fructify each other and creation arises anew.

Through our modern life-style we have cut ourselves off from these natural cycles. We have forgotten to listen to the cosmic rhythm of ebb and flow and its in breath and out breath of light. The degree in which we are attuned harmoniously to these daily and yearly cycles can be measured in the vitality, health and happiness we manifest in body, soul and mind.

What the lower kingdoms do unconsciously, man, as the synthesis of all creation, is called to do consciously. Our task is the mastery, direction, and harmonization of energy. We do well to remember that there is only one and the same Universal Life Force in everyone and in everything that exists, and that the fabric of creation is activating spirit energy on one side and receptive formative life force on the other side. Their uniting gives rise to all.

The cosmic rhythm and its influence of in breathing and out breathing of energy throughout the year brings into our awareness that there are "power points" at the cusps of the seasons where one season turns into the next. In ancient times people celebrated these points by holding Solar- or Fire-festivals of three days' duration. They understood that the celebration of the festivals at the cusps of the seasons would activate the Earth energies and unite them with the creative spiritual energy from the Cosmos, piercing the power points like spears of light. Thereby the ancients helped the Sun and Earth energies to unite and create light.

In antiquity the main task of priests was the cultivation and ordering of the seasonal festivals. They set the tone for the celebration of these festivals. They gave them their content. In so doing the priests themselves felt this content very deeply and, by their genuine enthusiasm, amplified and distributed the inspiring and invigorating effect of the festivals among the people at large. Thus, in celebrating the Solsticial and Equinoxial festivals, the profundity and meaning of this harmony between man, nature and spirit was experienced in body, soul and mind. The consciousness of the people was attuned with the rhythm of Nature, and participation in a festival permeated with spirit not only what they saw and heard around them but also what they experienced with their whole being. Thus people realised the weaving of the spiritual in the successive changes of outer nature, in growth and decline, in waxing and waning, and they experienced inward harmony with the celestial symphony and lived in close relationship with it.

Man must once more learn to "think" the spiritual rhythm underlying the natural cycles of his life. By accomplishing this, he will know how to live in harmony as a mediator between the spiritual energies of heaven and earth. Then life will awaken to joy for him. Albert Einstein once expressed similar thoughts:

A human being is a part of the whole called by us the Universe, a part limited in time and space. He experiences himself, his thoughts, his feelings, as something separate from the rest — a kind of optical delusion of his consciousness. The delusion is a kind of prison for us, restricting us to our personal desires and to affection for a few persons nearest to us. Our task must be to free ourselves from this prison by widening our circle of compassion to embrace all living creatures and the whole of nature in its beauty. Nobody is able to achieve this completely, but striving for such achievement is in itself a part of the liberation and a foundation for inner security and harmony.

The Art of Living

And even if I knew that the whole world was to end tomorrow, I would go ahead and plant an apple tree!

— *Martin Luther*

Not everyone has the talent to make a living as an artist. However, each one of us is imbued with the same seed of talent for the most distinguished and rarest of all the arts: the art of living — the art of LIFE. It seems as if life itself has an innate urge for the widest possible dissemination of its blessings as its goal in man.

Much has been said and written about the purpose and meaning of life. In the end of all the searching for a satisfactory answer to the mystery of life we arrive at the conclusion that life cannot be explained and understood in any other way than by consciously saying "Yes" to it in the actuality of the here and now at every moment and within all circumstances.

A man once travelled to India to meet a celebrated Guru. The old Master received him with the typical introductory words: "Do you have a question?" The teacher in this tradition always answers questions. He doesn't tell you anything you are not yet ready to hear.

The man answered: "Yes, I have a question. Since everything in the universe is a manifestation of divinity itself, how should we say 'No' to anything in the world? How should we say 'No' to brutality, to stupidity, to vulgarity, to thoughtlessness?"

The Master answered: "For you and for me, the way is to say 'Yes' at all times."

It is easy to affirm life when things go well according to our own wishes and desires. But how do we joyously affirm life when things apparently go against us? In short, how do we master life? The secret to mastery of life begins with the radical new insight, usually gained only after repeated suffering, that life is not what you thought it was!

The affirmation of all manifestations of life is the recognition of the eternal dimension, the divine essence, as the only essence of all that is. Our challenge is to see "through" the transitory world of appearances and recognize this eternal divine essence which IS and IS NOW the only reality that ever was, is, and ever will be — where all things just ARE. Thereby spiritual consciousness is realized by recognizing that there is just ONE DIVINE LIFE manifesting as your true SELF, your neighbour's SELF, and all other SELVES.

The sayings: "Let Go and let God", and "Just breathe and believe", imply: "Let God and let LIFE.....BE!"

The more you co-operate and accept the gift of life with gratitude, the more harmony and beauty you will perceive behind all manifestations, and realize in your own life. Then your life will bear fruit and start to prosper. The wholehearted AFFIRMATION of LIFE from you in answer to the gift of life marks the most important step on the path of mastery of the art of living.

Has there ever been a time when you felt as if there was a magic force weaving the threads of your life's events more harmoniously into a pattern of meaning? Did it seem as if there were invisible helpers guarding and guiding you along your path and helping you in a situation when you were most desperate and had given up all hope?

The appearance of these "miracles" in your life is the realization of the fact that you are attuned to the cosmic harmony, that you have united yourself with the rhythm of life's flow. It proves that you have accepted the truth that you are not a separate life squeezed into a limited life-span between birth and death, but that instead you are an inseparable part in the chain of the ONE LIFE, the ONE BEING, whom we all are. This is the proof that you have let this ONE LIFE live itself and be manifested through you.

Once you have allowed this to happen and realized the benefit of doing so, it must naturally occur to you that this is the way it should be all the time. A little honest introspection will reveal that you must have been habitually preventing it from happening all the time. The obvious goal then becomes the total abandonment of the attempt to manipulate life to conform to your ideas of what it should be like. Total surrender equals total freedom. How simple the whole thing really is!

The news media constantly bombard us with rumours and tidings of wars, suicide bombings, disease epidemics, and other catastrophes. Yet every minute, somewhere on the planet, life is newly affirmed by the unheralded arrival of a newborn child. Children are the real act of daring in a dangerous world. St. Paul wrote: "Ye must be as little children to enter into the Kingdom of Heaven". Dare to live! What a great affirmation of life is the birth of a baby born into a troubled world — a reminder of life's continuous everlasting flow beyond the human grasp of understanding.

As the Sun rises in the morning, so the human child arises from the nocturnal sea of unconsciousness and looks upon the wide, bright world which lies before it in a steadily expanding field of action caused by its own appearance. If the Sun were endowed with human feelings and consciousness, it would see as its fulfilment the widest possible dissemination of its blessings. So too the child pursues its unforeseen course to its zenith: unforeseen because its career is unique and individual. Its culminating point cannot be calculated in advance.

In the poem "Reflections" by the German author Hermann Hesse (1888-1962) the maternal principle is the expression of permanence and eternal rebirth; the paternal principle represents "the spirit". The poem begins with the line "Divine and Eternal is the Spirit" and continues:

> But nature does not satisfy
> The paternal spark of the immortal spirit
> Breaks through its mother-magic
> And leads the child to manhood,
> Extinguishes innocence and arouses us
> To arms and conscience.
> Thus between mother and father
> Thus between body and spirit
> Dallies creation's most fragile child,
> The trembling soul of man, capable of suffering
> As no other being, and capable of the very highest;
> Of believing, of loving hope

Spirit and Nature in constant alternation and tension ever create new forms in LIFE's limitless ventures and experiences.

When man accepts his own indestructible SELF, the seed of LIFE within himself, as an inseparable part of the ONE DIVINE SELF, the ONE INFINITE LIFE, then his life is in harmony with the LAW of LIFE. The art is perfected. Man has mastered the rarest of all arts — the art of LIVING. His life is the fruit of one branch which is connected to all the other branches which grow on the magnificent tree .... The TREE OF LIFE.

Feeling the Pulse of Life

I have come that they may have life, and have it to the full — *(John 10:10)*

When you hear these words of John, what are your thoughts about them? Look around you. Do you feel that we have life to the full? Or would you rather say, we have material things to the full?

Since the beginning of the 19th century mankind has set so much faith in scientific and technical progress that we often forget the price we pay for the "technical blessings" which have been showered upon us. We lose sight of our most valuable gift, Life!

There have always been a few warning voices which have tried to point to the many detrimental side-effects of the one-sided materialistic frame of thinking for the integrity of the human being and the life of this planet Earth.

Most of us are yearning for a different, more fulfilling life: but we don't know how to achieve that. In the end we find ourselves caught in a vicious cycle. The lack of meaning and contentment we feel is compensated with material things. As this gives only a temporary satisfaction, there will always be new cravings.

Man, the highest developed life-form, has also become the greatest threat to his own survival and the life of the Earth by wasting the resources of this planet and thus destroying the basis for his own life.

The other day, I found a study which says that the happiest people in the world are the people on the Island of Vanatu in the South-Pacific. The publisher of the local newspaper, an American, said: "The people here are happy because they are content with little. Their attention is centered around the community life, family and friends. They ask themselves: 'What can I contribute to the common good'?"

With these thoughts in mind at the beginning of this new year's cycle, I made a resolution to center my life more than ever around the care and nourishment of meaningful, affectionate human relationships — meeting people face to face, doing things together with others, and spending more time outdoors in nature. To start with, I am taking better care of my body and enhancing my own vitality. How can one appreciate and honour life while disregarding one's own body?

There is a tendency today to look at and treat the human body in a materialistic way. The natural body is not appreciated and accepted as it is but gets manipulated and either starved or overfed. In the worst case, surgeons have to cut and improve it as if it was a thing that could be fashioned according to popular trends.

Then there are people who regard themselves as more "enlightened". They want to give credit only to the spirit and soul. The human body is regarded as something of little value, that gets in the way of man's spiritual nature, and is to be overcome. They seem to forget that life's lessons cannot be learned in the head only. It is the threefold union of body, soul and spirit together which defines the human being. If we want to improve ourselves, we have to take all three aspects of our being into consideration and bring them into greater harmony.

This is also what Jesus Christ meant with resurrection of the body. It is the transformation and integration of body, soul and spirit into a higher life-form and level of consciousness. Few have understood the relationship between the threefold nature of man — the microcosm, and the trinity of God — the macrocosm.

The Greek philosophers introduced the idea of the eternal soul. The Christian Church adopted this philosophy and interpreted it to mean the resurrection of man as a resurrection of his soul. The physical body of man became associated with his sinful nature, which was the source of all evil. This thought of a sinful body is still slumbering in Western man's consciousness and gives way to an attitude that can only be called fear of living. Those persons in history, who claimed that *all* natural and individual life had to be affirmed, were persecuted by the Church as heretics. Fear of life and fear of God was preached from the Church's pulpits and the people were kept in ignorance of the true nature of their own being and that of the Universe. The original joyous message and testimony of Jesus that God is a living and loving Father either was not grasped or had been forgotten. Like children to a father, we can establish a personal relationship with, and experience the unitarian nature of man, God and the Universe. To the degree that man is able to understand and realize this unity in his life, so will he accomplish his personal spiritual evolution and be assured of his survival.

To feel the pulse of life anew, watch little children. Pay close attention to their enthusiasm as they learn to live, using all their senses. What a miracle life is! See, how they concentrate as they set one foot before the other or touch and taste the world around them. For them, happiness is just to be alive!

There is a fairy-tale called *Rumpelstiltskin* by the Brothers Grimm. Here the wicked wizard comes to the poor girl whom he has helped to become a princess to demand his payment. She offers him all the treasures of the kingdom, but he refuses everything.

"Let us talk about life", the wizard says. "I prefer something living to all the treasures and riches in the world".

To end, I wish to share with you some lines from *Peter Camenzind* by Hermann Hesse:

My intention was to familiarize man with the overflowing and silent life of nature. I wanted to teach him to listen to the earth's heartbeat, to participate in the life of nature, and not to overlook in the press of his own little destiny that we are not gods, not creatures of our own making, but children, parts of the earth and of the cosmic whole. I wanted to remind people that, like the songs of the poet and our night-time dreams, rivers, seas, drifting clouds, and storms are symbols and bearers of our yearnings, yearnings that embrace the earth and the heavens and whose object is the undiluted certainty of citizenship and the immortality of all living things...

But I also wanted to teach people to find the springs of joy and the waters of life through affectionate familiarity with nature. I wanted to preach the art of observation, walking and enjoying, finding pleasure in what is at hand. I wanted to make you open your ears to what the mountains and the green islands have to say; I wanted to make you see what an immensely varied and busy life there is, daily blooming and bubbling over, outside your homes and towns. I wanted to make you ashamed of knowing more about wars, fashion, gossip, literature, and the arts than you do about the Spring who displays her vigorous life outside your towns, or about the river that flows beneath your bridges, or the woods and the meadows that your railways pass through ... and I desired that you, perhaps happier people than me, should discover even greater joys.

The Song of Love, Joy and Happiness

Restless is my heart, O Lord, because Thy love hath inflamed it with such a desire that it cannot rest but in Thee alone.

— Nicolas de Cusa

The Song of Solomon is one of the world's most famous love poems.

The Beloved introduces herself:

"I am a rose of Sharon, a lily of the valleys."

And her Lover describes her:

"Like a lily among thorns is my darling among the maidens."

The Beloved says:

"Let him kiss me with the kisses of his mouth — for your love is more delightful than wine."

She expresses her passion:

"Strengthen me with raisins, refresh me with apples, for I am faint with love."

She imagines:

"His left arm is under my head, and his right arm embraces me."

What a passion! How profound the aching and yearning for her lover! She goes on:

> "My lover thrust his hand through the latch-opening; my heart began to pound for him."

We sense the fever of anticipation in the words. She continues:

> "I arose to open for my lover, and my hands dripped with myrrh, my fingers with flowing myrrh, on the handles of the lock."

> "I opened for my lover, but my lover had left; he was gone. My heart sank at his departure. I looked for him but did not find him. I called him but he did not answer."

What disappointment! But later, we know that there is to be a happy ending. The Beloved says:

> "My lover has gone down to his garden, to the beds of spices, to browse in the gardens and to gather lilies.

> "My lover is mine and I am his; he browses among the lilies.

> "Come away, my lover, and be like a gazelle or like a young stag on the spice-laden mountains."

We share the joy and happiness that is the outcome of this reunion, but also we learn that the fruit of this love is best consumed in freedom.

Today we find it difficult to understand the full meaning of the ancient language in this old love-poem. However, we sense the depth of the symbolism of the red rose brought together with the white lily and we feel it working upon our soul and calling forth profound feelings that resonate with our whole being.

What is it that is described here in such colourful imagery? We cannot help but get the impression that it is not so much about two lovers as a metaphorical description of the yearning of the human soul for reunion with its transcendental source, the divine Unity.

This is a theme that recurs in all mystical literature: the connection the soul seeks with the Infinite Mind, the ONE, the ALL. Sometimes it is compared to the erotic flame of a burning heart. The fulfilment of this love is sometimes called "The Mystical Wedding", when all feelings of separateness dissipate and a union of Creation and Creator takes place. This experience is also referred to as "Enlightenment" when, in an instantaneous clarity of perception, the universal existence as eternal life is recognized.

In this Greater Light, the true meaning of Light, Life and Love are seen as different aspects of the Divine Unity. This vision is described as the most intense realization of joy and happiness and love a man can reach on earth.

In the aftermath, a new sense of perception and understanding is developed. It is as if one could see all things as what they really are in their essence rather than in their outer appearances.

Having once come close to this condition of perfect peace, goodness and wisdom, man will know that he has come "home" at the end of a long journey. His searching and longing are ended.

All fears disappear: even the fear of death vanishes. Man is now reborn in "holiness". He understands the nature of sin, but he no longer sees that there is any sin in the world from which to escape.

Man sees that the life which radiates through him is eternal as all life is eternal, that the soul of man is immortal as God is. Freedom is conferred by this realisation.

This vision conveys an understanding that all things work together for the good of each and all. Its "Illumination" brings about a veritable "transfiguration" of man. This is what the poet Dante means, when he says he was "transhumanized into God".

In the depths of our being we hear the whispers of the Divine inspiration. With each breath we take, we feel the connection with the breath of THE WHOLE, the foundation of all love.

Sometimes we can catch a glimpse of the mystery of this new state of being when we are in the beginning of a loving relationship with another person. However, we realise in the end that it is but a colourless image of that fulfilment, that essence of pure love and truth, of which the "Song of the Song" speaks to our soul.

This is what the mystics of all ages have tried to tell us about the awakening of the soul to the awareness of the Divine Life and Love. As one of the greatest Jewish mystics of the thirteenth century, Abraham Abulafia, described this experience:

> Now we are no longer separated from our source, and behold we are the source and the source is us. We are so intimately united with IT, we cannot by any means be separated from IT, for we are IT.

It is the secret of the Divine Love that it is hidden within our soul. It is always with us, but until we start to look for it there, we will never find it.

St. John of the Cross said:

> The soul of one who serves the God within always swims in joy, always keeps a holiday, is always in a palace of jubilation, ever singing with fresh ardour and fresh pleasure a new song of joy and love.

We do not have to search for God, for God is all that is; it permeates and sustains the Universe. If there is a search, then God is searching for itself.

To commence your search for Love, Truth and Happiness, visualize yourself joining all the seekers through the ages, travelling back in time to

Greece, arriving at the gates of the Apollo Temple in Delphi, where you see the inscription written above the portal:

"KNOW THYSELF — AND YOU WILL KNOW THE GOD WITHIN YOU."

It is an old saying that the more the soul is longing and preparing itself to receive the Divine, the more the Divine reaches down to meet the soul.

Then the soul will recognise that there is no difference between the seeker and the goal of the search. The lover and the beloved are one with the source of their love.

As St Paul put it:

For now we see through a glass darkly: then we shall see face to face. Now I know in part; then I shall know fully, even as I am fully known.

To Love or Not to Love...

Seek thee the Grail for the healing of our wounded time.

— Anonymous

There lived once in China a wise old woman, who had taken care of a young monk for more than 20 years. She had built a hut up in the mountain for him and taken care of all his needs. Thus the monk was free to devote himself to his spiritual study and meditation only.

As the years passed and the woman grew older, she did not know how much longer she would be able to provide for the monk. She decided to find out what kind of progress he had made in his spiritual development during his years of study and meditation. Therefore, she sent a young attractive girl up to the mountain with a gift and she told her to express much affection for him, to embrace him, and all of a sudden to ask, "What now?"

The young girl climbed up the mountain to visit the monk and did all the woman had told her to do. She hugged him and caressed him with great affection and then asked all of a sudden, "What now?"

"An old tree grows on a cold rock in winter", replied the monk in a poetic manner. "There is no warmth far or near."

The girl returned from her trip and reported what had happened and what the monk had said to her.

"When I consider that I have fed this fellow for more than 20 years!" the old woman shouted, very upset. "He showed no empathy, no heart or

33

understanding for your feelings. Nobody asked him to share your passion, but at least he could have shown *compassion* for you."

Immediately, the old woman went up the mountain and burned down the monk's hut.

When you embark on a spiritual quest, you learn the importance of developing certain habits and virtues. Also, you will find out for yourself that without discipline and persistence, and without setting aside enough time for meditation and regular periods of withdrawal from the distraction of the mundane world you won't get very far. This is of the greatest value, and often requires much sacrifice from you in many forms.

Therefore it is recommended that you create or find a place, a sanctuary, where you can sit in peace to prepare yourself for the quest to ascend the highest mountain a human being can climb, the Mount Everest of his own soul.

Today more and more spiritual seekers feel this inner urge, "the itch that cannot be scratched"; and each wonders: "Who am I? Am I really this personality? Is my life, all that I've been through, all there is?" Thus the quest begins.

These questions formed the foundation for a development that Rudolf Steiner called the "New Age". Over the years, this movement has grown into a prospering worldwide market which claims to provide the means for the ever-growing flock of seekers to achieve "enlightenment", or a higher state of consciousness, by means of all kinds of tools, books, music, shamanic tours, prophet conferences, etc.

This overload of information on spirituality brings about a sort of *fear* in the seeker, who is liable to experience diffuse feelings of insecurity and confusion, of perhaps missing something important, of not finding the right *guru* who knows all the answers, of not following the "right" path, as there are so many. Some seekers may also fear "wasting" time on pursuing a particular path if a shorter alternative path can be found.

Like other businesses, the "New Age" conferences with the well-known names of so-called spiritual leaders and guides are not inexpensive: they follow the old rule that people are liable think that what does not cost much is not worth much.

The lure of commercial profit has found entrance to and corrupted the spiritual movement. Instead of telling the seeker that he needs only to study the one single book which he himself is, that only within himself can he find all the answers to his questions, he is tempted to acquire more and more "knowledge" in the form of books, tapes, videos; by attending more seminars, and by purchasing more memberships in obscure groups or cults.

After the enormous growth of mankind's technological facilities for satisfying our material desires, the "prince of this world" is tempting us now with the poison fruit of "Knowledge for Knowledge's sake" even on the spiritual path. Never in history has there been so much access to "knowledge": yet it is hard to demonstrate that it has helped to free the individual or the collective from their most urgent problems.

Above all else, the state of the world today manifests *fear*. It is the underlying ground of most of our problems. What is missing? Where is the TRUTH that can free us from fear?

"What now?" asked the young girl in the story with which we began.

"Our deepest fear is not that we are inadequate", said Nelson Mandela in his poem, *'Fear'*. "Our deepest fear is that we are powerful beyond measure. It is our light, not our darkness, that most frightens us."

We are AFRAID to LOVE. This is the answer. Why? Because we don't know what Love is. If we knew love we would not be afraid of it. Obviously what we *thought* love was is nothing but ego-love, a mere surrogate, which doesn't take away our fear permanently.

We think the world is the problem: but the world is only manifesting what we are. When we want a different world, we have to change ourselves. We have all heard this so often, but did we change inside?

Could it be that we heard the words, but didn't pay attention because we preferred to stay in our prison? Our prison is a known quantity; at least we feel safe there. What comes in and goes out is strictly controlled. We are accustomed to Inertia. All stays the same. We feel "secure" locked up in our familiar fear as in a tomb.

However we don't give up our fantasizing that something might happen, some day, and we might find love. We may even hope for it. But how can love find us, when we don't open the door that separates us from it?

Why are we afraid to love? Because we have misconstrued our true essence and nature by identifying with our ego-selves. We have forgotten who we are. We do not realise that we ourselves are holding the door shut from the inside, and so insulating ourselves from the love we want so desperately.

The world is not the problem. We, ourselves, are not the problem. Our false beliefs are the problem! Allowing Truth to correct our false beliefs ends the problem. The truth is that our essence, our true nature, our true Self, *is* LOVE. When we realise this, our only task is to overcome our fears and obstacles; to jump out of our self-created ego-prison and express the freedom of our true Self, which is united with the Infinite, the divine LOVE.

The way most of us live reminds me of the story where a man has devoted his entire life to study the mystery of love. Then one day love knocks on his door and the man, deep in his studies, shouts: "Go away! I have no time. I'm searching for love". And so love goes away....

A Lesson in Love

Set me as a seal upon your heart.
As a ring upon your arm;
For love is strong as death....
Its flashes are flashes of fire.
A flame of the Eternal.

— Song of Songs

All the world's spiritual traditions convey the same message: True love, the highest form of love, is experienced when you are able to sacrifice yourself and rise to that insight that reveals that you are a mirror image of your surroundings. It is the mystical experience of oneness. Other beings are true reflections of your own higher self. It is the realization that you must find the other in yourself — THOU ART THAT!

To recognize the other in yourself is also the theme of the romantic fable *The Disciple at Sais* written by the German mystic Novalis. In it the hero is a young, good, but extremely odd fellow called Hyacinth, a loner who used always to brood about strange things. Hyacinth received a book from a stranger and was overwhelmed by a burning love for the Mother of all Things, the Virgin with the Veil, the Goddess Isis. He left his country, forgot about his beautiful beloved maiden, Rosebud, and set out on a long journey during which his whole nature was gradually transformed. One day he fell asleep, for only Dream could lead him into the Holy of Holies. At last he stood before the celestial virgin. He lifted the thin glistening veil... What did he see? Miracle of miracles — he saw Rosebud!

THOU ART THAT!

The Philosopher Schopenhauer, in his essay *On the Foundations of Morality*, posed the question: "How is it possible that suffering which is neither my own nor of my concern should immediately affect me as though it were my own, and with such force that it moves me to action?"

This is something really mysterious, something for which reason can provide no explanation, and for which no basis can be found in practical experience. It is not unknown even to the most hard-hearted and self-interested. Examples abound of the instant response of one person helping another, coming to his aid without reflection, even setting his own life in clear danger for someone whom he sees for the first time, having nothing more in mind than that the other is in need or in peril of his life.

Schopenhauer's answer was that the immediate reaction and response represented the breakthrough of a metaphysical realization which is best described by Thou Art That. "This presupposes", Schopenhauer wrote, "his identification with someone not himself, a penetration of the barrier between persons so that the other was no longer perceived as a separate person from oneself but as a person in whom I suffer, in spite of the fact that his skin does not enfold my nerves".

This fundamental insight reveals, according to Schopenhauer, that "my own true inner being, the eternal Self, exists in every living creature ... and is the ground of that compassion upon which all true, that is to say, unselfish, virtue rests, and whose expression is in every good deed".

Some time ago I participated in a philosophical discussion group where many distinguished people excelled themselves in lively debates. During one of these discussions, when everyone had made his point, suddenly a man lifted his arm to make a contribution. It was the first time I had noticed this man as he had kept himself completely in the background. Somehow he did not seem to fit into this circle of scholars. Now, as he raised his voice, everybody turned around and looked at the man, which seemed to make him feel uncomfortable. He searched for words in such a way that you knew he was not used to speaking in public. This is what he had to contribute:

> "From all that I have experienced in life", he said, "I have come to the conclusion that it is love alone that provides a key to the profound philosophical question of 'What is the meaning of life?'. It is love that enriches the blood of one's own life with understanding and wisdom. The true nature of each person is in fact his or her own selfless realization of that love and understanding. It is not mere verbalization, but an actual demonstration of love. And this love is not for oneself only. By unfolding it through our actions we all fructify more and more, simultaneously, both our neighbour's life and our own."

There was only silence after the man had finished. No one said anything. And gradually the group dispersed. The man has not been seen since.

When I heard these words, it reminded me of another story — and I would like to share it with you.

A soldier, named Jack, said to his commanding officer: "My friend isn't back from the battlefield, Sir. Request permission to go out and get him."

"Permission refused", said the officer. "I don't want you to risk your life for a man who is probably dead."

The soldier went out all the same, and, an hour later, came back mortally wounded, carrying the corpse of his friend.

The officer was furious. "I told you he was dead. Now I've lost both of you. Tell me, was it worth going out there to bring in a corpse?"

The dying man replied, "Oh, it was, Sir. When I found him, he was still alive. He looked at me and said: 'Jack, I was sure you'd come!'"

Harvesting the Golden Fruit

I cannot forget, but I can forgive — *Nelson Mandela*

Every year at the time of the Autumn equinox people garnish their homes and altars with the best fruits of the harvest. In many countries it has become a habit to carve a face in a reddish-golden pumpkin and set it on the doorstep. Lit by a candle from the inside it has become a symbol for the Thanksgiving season and a token that we can trust in the merciful and bountiful nature of the Universe.

There is another tradition, called *Samhain* or "All Hallows Eve", in which an effigy, representing our "old self", is placed on a bon-fire (good fire) so that it may be consumed by the flames and thereby release its light.

This act manifests a process of transformation and resurrection to bless the community and the land. Contemplating the effigy's gradual changes and how it is consumed by the bonfire calls our attention to those things in our own lives which need purification. What is it that we don't want to see in ourselves, lest we project it on to others? What are the negative feelings, (like criticism, envy, fear, jealousy, pride or resentment) we still harbour, although we know that they stand in the way of our soul's development? It might surprise us much later to find out that these stumbling blocks have actually turned into stepping stones on the path of the mastery of the "Wheel of Life".

The Sun's annual cycle through each of the twelve zodiacal signs mirrors our own soul's journey on its evolutionary path. The astrological constellations represent twelve phases of the Universal Life energy. Each of them has its own particular effect on us and provides us with a challenge necessary to "straighten out" our character and prepare us for higher development.

The Greek myth of Hercules comes to mind. Twelve labours were given him by Eurystheus as a means of redemption from his sins before he could regain his status as Sun-Hero and immortal being. His eleventh task was to gather the "golden apples" from the Garden of the Hesperides. This was a realm of the power of the goddess and related particularly to Athena, the virgin-goddess of wisdom. After a long and perilous search Hercules finally succeeded in finding the garden. Using all his powers and wits he retrieved the golden apples. He took them to Eurystheus who granted him mercy and told him to keep the golden apples as a gift. However, Hercules decided not to keep the apples for himself but instead offered them to the goddess Athena. Finally, Athena carried them back to the Garden of the Hesperides where they originated.

What are these "golden apples" from the Garden of the Goddesses? It is said that the word 'Hesperides' means "in the far West". Here we have a garden with golden apples and the feminine principle in the West. On the other side we might remember the biblical garden that was planted by God himself in the Eastern side of Eden. One interpretation of that story tells that the eating of the apple from the "Tree of Good and Evil" brought about the fall into a lower plane of consciousness and the exit from Eden.

Obtaining the golden apples from the Garden of the Goddesses points to another tree, the Tree of Life, which is a symbol of Eternal Life. To lay hold of the fruit of this tree is the master-key on the path of return for the hero in the myth. It unlocks the door to higher understanding of the principles of the spiritual world and prepares the way for re-integration with the Divine Source. This return journey of the hero, of

Hercules, is also our own soul's journey on which each one of us will one day embark in the search and harvest of the "golden fruit".

A great stumbling-block on everyone's spiritual path is the seedling of guilt and sin, which has taken root in the Western collective consciousness due to a mis-interpretation of the biblical story of the Fall. As these feelings are unconscious they are very difficult to access and release.

What all wisdom teachings reveal, and what is at the heart of all religions, is that the Truth of forgiveness, compassion and loving-kindness is the fulcrum upon which the entire Universe is balanced. Wherever mercy is practised, the beauty, the harmony, and the wisdom of the Universe shine forth.

As a little gift for you to remember this moment I would like to share with you a story from the Jewish wisdom teachings. It says in this story that in the service of God there are accusing and defending angels. If the defending angels did not do their job well, the world would not continue. Therefore God gives the defending angels a task to prepare them and deepen their understanding.

God said: "Go find the most excellent quality of human experience, and return to tell me what it is".

The angel sent on the task searched and searched and came back with two examples of human goodness and bravery: willingness to sacrifice one's life for another; and the pain of a woman giving birth, i.e. bringing life into the world.

But God answered the angel: "These are indeed examples of excellent human behaviour, but neither is the most excellent one. Try one more time."

So the angel again returned to the world and searched very carefully; being an angel, it could view thousands of events at the same time. Suddenly something caught its attention — a man running through a wooded area, clearly in a violent mood. The angel quickly reviewed this man's life and found that he had just been released from jail, having served many years for another man's crime. Now, furious, he was out for revenge. The angel followed him through the woods and saw him approach a cabin in which lived the guilty one who should have served the prison term.

When the running man came close to the house, he saw a light shining through the window. Standing at the window, still bent on revenge, he looked inside and saw his intended victim. The man and his bride of one year had just returned from the hospital with their new daughter. They were as happy as people can be. As the angry man watched, his heart slowly broke into pieces. He began to weep, and turned away into the woods, never to return.

May we all be encouraged and inspired by this story. May we live the seasons of our lives confident in the promise that each one of us will participate in the harvest of the golden fruit of wisdom. Once we have found this wisdom we shall know what to do: we must offer it in service to the world and give it back to the source from whence it came.

Non nobis, non nobis, sed Nomine Tuo da gloriam — Not for us, Lord, not for us, but to Thy name be the glory.
(Psalm 115, verse 1)

The Peace that Passeth all Understanding...

Two things fill my mind with ever new and increasing wonder and awe,
the more often and the more constantly reflection concentrates upon
them: The starry heaven above me and the moral law within me.

— *Immanuel Kant (1724-1804)*

Looking up to the starry heaven since primordial times, man must
have felt in his own heart a resonance of his inner essence with the
harmony and peace of the cosmic. Thus the spiritual impulse
found expression and made man erect the first altar. From that time on,
man was on his way home. Although often only dimly felt inside, he
yearns to be integrated back into the COSMIC Order, because he feels
that this is his true SOURCE and ORIGIN.

On this search man has explored and conquered his outer world, but
not been able to feel "at home" in it. Now he wonders why, in all his
mastery of the external world, he has never been able to live in peace with
his fellow beings on this planet.

Man doesn't know who he is or why he is here or how he can live in peace.

When man decides to search for the meaning of his existence, he
changes his direction from the horizontal to the vertical dimension. He
begins to explore the inner world of his consciousness. He tries to find
within himself that peace he was never able to establish in the outer
world. This inner peace is described in the sacred texts as "the PEACE

which transcends our understanding". It seems to be a mark of all religious endeavours and be true for all human beings.

We often experience a stage of profound peace at night. In deep sleep, when our personal identity is forgotten, we find a peace that is much different from our waking state. It seems that when the outer personality, the ego, is not active we enter into a realm of peace and joy; a state in which the body repairs and rejuvenates itself. Now we ask: Who is the experiencer and who is the witness in deep sleep? There must be "something" because, when we wake up, we are still aware of this state. Who is there? Who am I, when I don't identify with my outer personality? I don't cease to be..... Something is there although I don't quite know what it is.

Every morning when we "think" we wake up, we actually fall "asleep" to our higher Self and identify again with our outer self. We "fall" back into a lower vibrational plane which we call the material world.

Here we approach a mystery. We seem to have two identities: a "me" which identifies us with our body; and another "I" which, whatever it is, is not bound to the material world.

Once you have noticed that you can observe the "me" and distinguish it from the observing "I", your view of "reality" changes. You have discovered your higher Self. Now you have a choice: With which Self will you identify? Will you be able to release the conditioning thoughts about the "me" you "thought" you were and take the leap into the vast unknown world of your own unrestricted unconsciousness? You can read and listen to what others who have travelled the same path might tell you "about" that journey, but you will never know unless you perform that act of ultimate self-sacrifice and re-identify with your spiritual Self.

How can this state of calm and profound PEACE which is experienced in deep sleep be maintained and experienced consciously in the waking state?

Re-member you are a spiritual being, a part of a Spiritual Infinite Consciousness, which is manifesting as the "I" in you and as the "I" in me. It is the same ONE DIVINE CONSCIOUSNESS expressing ITSELF everywhere. If we could only awaken from our sleep of separation and limitation, we should realise the vastness of the Universe which is our real Self.

The more we are able to let go of our attachment to our outer selves and acknowledge our spiritual inner SELF, the higher we shall rise into the spiritual realms. We can do so by QUESTIONING EVERYTHING. Asking WHAT IS? and accepting the answers we receive are two sides of the same coin? We gradually come to learn that the spiritual realm is a world of PEACE, ORDER AND HARMONY, where all opposites are united into ONENESS. Under the guidance of our inner Self, we shall experience that PEACE which passeth all understanding.

To bring forth in us and through us the PEACE of the Spirit, it is necessary to be still in mind and body, so that in that silence the rhythm of the universe can flow forth as harmony. Listen to the still voice inside you: BE STILL AND KNOW that I AM!

In the Russian language the word "Mir" is synonymous with peace and the Universe. Here we have the touchstone for the truth. The Universe and peace are indivisible, because their essence is of a spiritual nature. There is ONE spiritual Universe which IS Peace and Harmony.

Peace Profound is a characteristic of the Universe, the INFINITE, the COSMIC, "MIR" and "mir". The peaceful endeavor of the spirit of man is united in ONE and the same CONSCIOUSNESS with the UNIVERSE. This whole universe is simply the objectification of a single causal agent. This causal agent is GOD. The "something" in you that says "I AM" is identical with the "something" in me that says "I AM". We are not GOD, but we are GOD exiled for a little while into the forgetfulness of our true SELF, yet soon to awaken to the full measure of our splendour and glory. When we realize our inner spiritual SELF, we finally understand that we are immortal and eternal.

I feel the air of other spheres...

I dissolve into tones, circling, wreathing...
Yielding involuntarily to the great breathing....
The earth shakes, white and soft as foam.
I climb across huge chasms.
I feel as if I were swimming beyond the farthest cloud
In a sea of crystalline brilliance.
I am only a flicker of sacred fire.
I am only a mumbling of the sacred voice.

Stefan George (German poet 1868 - 1933)

◄ ✿ ➤

The Meaning of Charity

Charity to be fruitful must cost us. ...to love, it is necessary to give: to give it is necessary to be free from selfishness.

— *Mother Teresa of Calcutta*

When we hear the word "charity" we think of love towards our neighbour, love made visible as in service. We hear the word everyday; we use it and we may also practise it in different forms.

But what does charity really mean? According to the definition of charity as love towards the neighbour we need to find out first what loving means to us at this very moment.

We are not interested in ideas about love or wish to repeat what we have heard or read about it. The word is so loaded and corrupted that we often don't feel comfortable using it. So let us wash away all the definitions and concepts that have been imposed on us by the outer world. The answer lies deep within us. Love is the essence of what and who we are. This strange flower blooms in the stillness of the mind, but we run around searching for it in the outer world.

If we do not come upon this source, this well of love, within us and start to draw the living force out of its abundance — if we are not filled with it — the world will continue to stumble along. The task is to consciously let it stream through us unto everyone we come in touch with. We know intellectually that the unity of mankind is essential and that love is the only way to heal the world: but we don't know what love really is, and therefore we cannot put it into action.

The nature of love is always to reach beyond self. It is not satisfied with loving self, but it strives to love others and be united to others. Love acknowledges the differences between people, but is also the integrating force that overcomes separation. You feel another person's joy as joy in yourself. It does NOT mean feeling one's own joy in someone else. That is selfishness, loving oneself; the former is loving the neighbour. These two kinds of love are exact opposites. Both do form a bond, and it does not look as though loving oneself in someone else divides. However, it does separate — so much so that someone who has been loved in this way often later comes to respond with hatred. In fact, this bond gradually dissolves of its own accord.

We see therefore how what people often take for love is in fact only using the other to compensate for one's own lack of inner security, whether expressed as dependency, vanity, or desire for personal aggrandizement.

It is similar with charity. Remember what Mother Teresa said: "To truly give charity, you must be free of selfishness!"

It is pure joy of giving, which includes much more than material things. This givingness can have many faces, like in a warm smile to strangers, a personal thank-you-letter, an encouraging hug, an unexpected phone call, a thoughtful word of appreciation, a bonding with a person in grief, a prayer for the healing of others, a heartfelt forgiving when you are wronged. All this is done not out of duty or responsibility but out of the abundance of warmth and love you feel welling up inside you. And the more you give out, the more flows back in; that is the joy of love in action, the manifestation of charity. As long as you feel compelled to do something because it is your duty or because you want something in return, there is no love.

When one truly loves there must be freedom, not only from the other person but from oneself. Charity can come into being only when there is total self-abandonment. It does not come as the result of any effort. Like a flower that spreads its perfume, it blooms for everybody. Whether one is near or far away, it is all the same to the flower because it is full of that fragrance and shares it with everybody.

Have you ever experienced moments of epiphany in your life? Mostly they happen unexpectedly. You listen to someone talking and you feel that your mind is drifting off to other thoughts, as our mind does all the time. Suddenly — something within us seems to ring a bell; we become alert, and in this awareness one sentence we have just overheard pierces our consciousness like a spear and there is an inner response like an influx of light, clarity and beauty. Suddenly you "know" what you just heard is Truth!

Such a moment happened to me when I heard someone saying that "maybe the meaning of our cycling from birth to birth is nothing else but learning the lessons of love". In that instant I knew that I had just been given a most valuable key: the key to the meaning of the annual cycle. It is the great labour of perfecting love in the cycles of a life-time. In the same manner as we witness it in the annual cycle in nature, with the dormant seed resting in the earth in winter, awakening in springtime, flowering in summer, and manifesting the mature fruit in autumn.

During these cycles, the dormant seed of human nature gradually transforms into higher and higher levels of perfection until finally a spiritual impulse awakes, desire turns into the will to love, selfish thoughts are transformed into greater understanding of what love means, and the fruit of this love is expressed in the manifestation of charity.

However, many lessons have to be learned before selfishness is transformed into the ability to truly love others. There is no greater mystery than the mystery of love itself. Mother Teresa said: "I do not think I have any special qualities. I don't claim anything for the work. It is His work. I am like a little pencil in His hand, that is all. He does the thinking. He does the writing. The pencil has nothing to do with it. The pencil has only to allow itself to be used."

Autumn is the time of harvesting the fruits of our endeavours. Have we been good gardeners? Let us celebrate together as we harvest the golden fruit, which is the manifestation of love in action. And let us not hoard the fruits for ourselves but be ready to share with others not only the fruits of our labours but also what we have learnt of the secrets of good gardening.

The challenge remains for all of us: May our life become a spark in the flame of charity, so that the warmth and light of this loving fire may shine ever more brightly and sustain hope in the hearts of mankind.

When the Light breaks Through....

Grace strikes us when we are in great pain and restlessness... Sometimes at that moment a wave of light breaks into our darkness, and it is as though a voice were saying: "You are accepted".

— *Paul Tillich*

It is in the time of winter, when the daylight is scarce and the darkness takes more and more space, that we seem most open, most receptive to our spiritual nature. It is also in the winter of our soul, when we suffer hardships or are under great tribulations, that we become receptive to an influx of light. In such a moment, a moment of grace and wonder, a wave of light breaks into our darkness and awakens us to a new life.

I would like to share a story with you. It is a true story, which happened exactly as I'm going to tell. Please come and accompany me on a time travel back to the events of that night...

It was a dark winter night in Sweden — a day before Christmas Eve. The young girl who waited at the small railway station was young and inexperienced. She had never travelled by herself — especially not at night on a train. And the tickets for the train's sleeping compartment were all sold out.

She was eagerly studying the faces and appearances of the other travellers who were waiting together with her for the train to arrive. It was an unusually cold night. Hopefully the train would be well heated and there would be nice company.

She decided to be very careful to pick the right compartment and find trustworthy company as she had to travel all night long. When the train arrived she took a seat beside some elderly ladies who seemed to be good-natured and quite talkative. A long night's journey through the night began.

As the hours passed, the train became quite empty; more and more travellers disembarked. There came a moment when the girl realized that she was the only traveller left in her compartment. The train's monotonous rocking movements made her feel as if she were drifting along drowsily. The interior light was sparse. She fell asleep.

All of a sudden the door of the compartment flew open. A huge man's torso appeared before the startled girl and a deep voice asked if it was allowed to take a seat. A stab of fear set the girl's heart pounding. Why, in all the world, did this old, big-bellied and shabbily dressed man have to get into her compartment?

How could she get out of here without offending him she pondered? She peered into the neighbouring compartments. Maybe she would see some people whom she could call in case the man were to molest her. But, there were no other people. All the neighbour compartments were empty. It seemed as if she was travelling in an empty train alone with this man. Completely discouraged, the girl crept back to her seat, which now seemed to be like a mousetrap to her.

Meanwhile, the stout man had made himself at home. His belongings were thrown all over the empty seats and soon he began unpacking some food, which he offered to share. The girl rejected his offer and turned her head gloomily away from his sight.

Then he rummaged again in his suitcase. Out came a bottle which was quickly uncorked with a loud "plop". The girl dared not to look at him. Obviously he was drinking alcohol and would soon be getting drunk. The man was enjoying himself thoroughly, taking one sip after the other and talking to himself. But he never forgot to offer to share a sip with her.

Time was passing and the girl sat silently, anxiously watching the man from the corner of her eyes, feeling helpless and utterly alone. She could not sit up any longer as the hours passed by. She felt the coldness of the night; her stiff body seemed to slide slowly down from the seat. She needed so badly to get some sleep.

Staring at her, the man encouraged her to lie down and take a nap. He would make some more space for her on the seats now occupied by his belongings. What was she to do?

As she couldn't stay awake any longer, she finally stretched out on the seats, turning her back to the man, so as not to see him any more. Still, her heart was pounding with fear. She remembered the scares that used to haunt her when she was a small girl. At that time, whenever she was afraid of being left alone in the dark, she had found for herself the secret of praying and talking to her guardian angel until she felt his presence surrounding her. If only she could remember the words of the prayer she used to say in those days when she was little.

And then she suddenly remembered and found herself murmuring the words of recognizing the presence of Jesus as being the good shepherd who was holding out his arms, folding and protecting his flock ever so tenderly. Holding fast to that vision, she felt a deep peace welling up inside her, and her breathing became more steady and calm.

But suddenly, she became wide awake again. Without opening her eyes, she felt the man noisily rise from his seat and begin to search in his luggage. He approached her. She dared not turn around, nor open her eyes, but caught her breath as she felt him coming closer and closer and... then she felt his hovering presence stooping down to her.

The man mumbled, "We don't want you to catch a cold during this ghastly night, sweet young lady. My coat will keep you warm and protect you". As he spoke, he bedded her down like you would do with a small child — carefully tucking the ends of the coat tightly around her. And he kept on whispering soothingly to her until she fell asleep.

Many years and many Christmas seasons have passed, but the memory of that night and that wave of light, of grace and of love that welled up in my heart and flooded my whole being will never leave me and has changed my life for ever.

It was the best Christmas gift I ever received.

AND THE LIGHT SHINETH...

"Into this happy night
In secret, seen of none,
Nor saw I aught,
Without other light or guide,
Save that which in my heart did burn."

— *St. John of the Cross*

What is the nature of this mysterious "light" to which St. John of the Cross refers in these lines and which he saw "burning" within his heart?

It is obviously not coming from an outside source, which means he is not speaking of a physical objective light. And this light is seen by no one but himself alone, which illustrates that he is in solitude — in meditation and stillness. Further, he speaks of the concentration of the will — of accepting no other light or guide than the fire of the divine wisdom alone, which is burning in the heart.

Let us share the joy of the moment when he becomes aware of this inner spiritual light, this "inner experience" by which one comes to see the spiritual light, which is also called the original light. This experience is often referred to as "enlightenment".

The ancients maintained that every sentient being possesses an original spiritual light drawn from "the Storehouse of the Great Divine Light". The "miracle light" of all the Buddhas is drawn from this same source. In our own lives, every single act of "seeing" is the marvellous work of that spiritual light of imagination. But ignorant man has forgotten this original light and turns to the outside in search of a worldly light.

To perceive this divine light in the soul means "to embark on life's supreme adventure" and find the greatest treasure that can be conferred upon the human soul on this earth. It is the recognition of the nature of our inner light, our soul-light, that burns within the deepest recesses of our consciousness. And until we have experienced this inner spiritual light, we will find no true joy, peace or happiness on earth.

Becoming aware of this inner light, which is the spark of Divinity within us and which lies hidden in the darkness of all matter, is the final purpose of our journey. All creation is seeking and striving towards the Light. "Seek the light" is an innate law and urge within all living creatures, especially those with some form of self-awareness. Truly dwelling in this Light of spiritual awareness every moment of our life will mark the culmination of our life's journey, the achievement of the soul's perfection on earth.

In the cycle of the zodiac, the annual rebirth of the Sun takes place at the winter solstice. The joyful event of the return of the light has given form in all cultures to many traditional ways of celebration. Christmas, as it is celebrated today in many countries of the world, has almost completely lost its deeper symbolical meaning. The profane world is mostly satisfied with traditional Christmas worship merely as an outward ceremony. For the majority of people, Christmas is just another commercial family feast which causes enormous stress and expense for all who participate in its celebration.

But we must remember that the mystical ceremonials of the pagan world and of the early Christians were but the outward symbols of inward processes. By the mystery of the Birth of Christ, the precious ideal of the perfection of the soul of man was transmitted from age to age.

So let us try to find a key that can help us unlock the door to the Christmas mystery and rediscover the spiritual dimension of its light.

Looking at the zodiacal cycle as a mirror of man's own soul transformation in going through 12 mighty labours, we can see the Birth of the Cosmic Christ as the incarnation of the Divine Light into the dark fallen world of matter.

This cosmic spark of light, the Christ impulse received into matter as redemptive energy, will — when unfolded in all aspects — lead men towards heights of endless realization. It is the mysterious irresistible drive of evolution toward perfection, revealing the father aspect. "Be perfect as our Father in Heaven"!

About this Light, that came into the world by the birth of the Christ, it is said: "And the LIGHT SHINETH in the darkness, but the darkness of the world understandeth it not...."

All theological revelations have to be contemplated on two different levels, one exoteric and another esoteric. To the literal minded, the Gospel is understood in an historic sense, preaching Jesus Christ and Him crucified; but to the mystic, burning with the love of Divine Wisdom, the Word — the impulse of the Christ — is alive within his own soul to quicken the work of transformation.

Let us contemplate the metamorphosis of a butterfly. In its unfoldment, the butterfly passes through three stages, like the three stages that the Jesus Christ of the Gospels experienced: Birth, Death and Resurrection.

Man is born naked, ignorant, and helpless. This birth is symbolized by the transformation of the egg into the larva.

The adolescent man, who is seeking truth and dwelling in meditation, is symbolized by the second transformation from larva to pupa, in which the insect enters its chrysalis (the tomb of the Mysteries).

The third transformation from pupa to imago (wherein the perfect butterfly comes forth — now unfolding the wings with which he may soar to the skies) is the completion of the work.

The Resurrection of the Christ typifies the unfolded and enlightened soul of man rising from the tomb of his lower nature (the body).

The threefold transformation of the butterfly is an allegory for the threefold mystery of the embodiment of the Christ, which represents the threefold transformation of our own soul's unfoldment.

When this great work is done, the gates of Universal Life will open. And the Kingdom of Heaven will welcome the newborn Sun-King, whose kingdom is not of this world.

And the LIGHT SHINETH forever... brightening the skies for gods immortal.

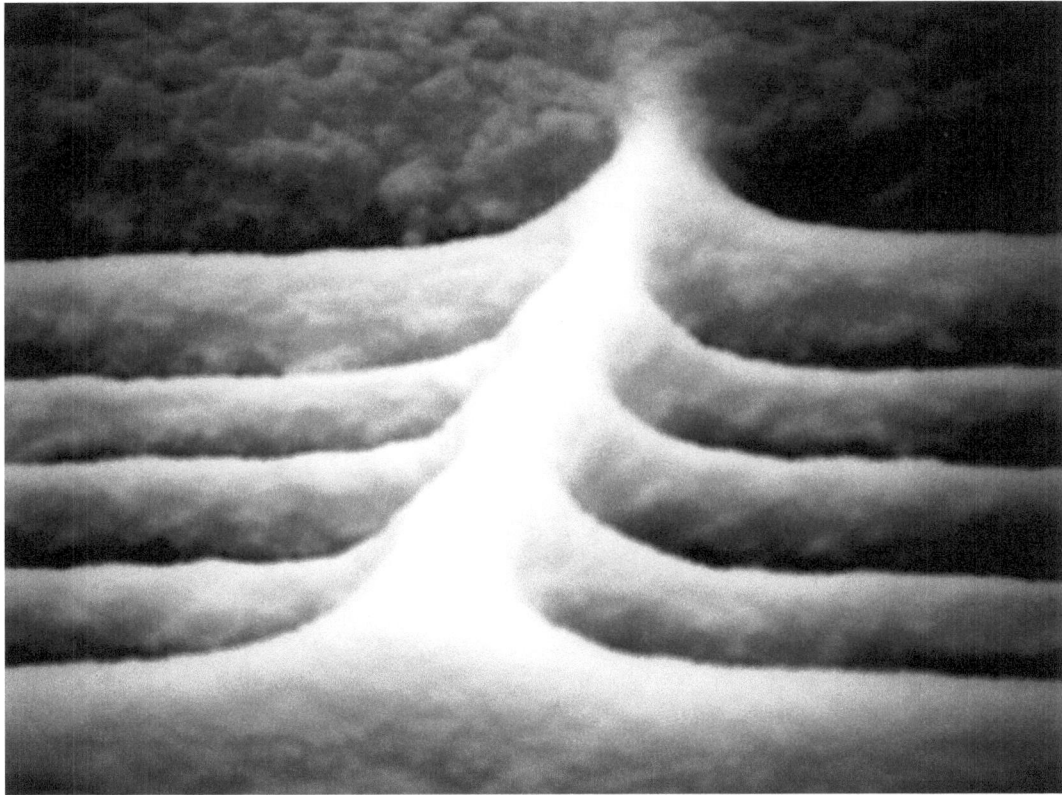

The Mystery of the Single Eye

The light of the body is the eye: if therefore thine eye be single, thy whole body shall be full of light. But if thine eye be evil, thy whole body shall be full of darkness. If therefore the light that is in thee be darkness, how great is that darkness!

— Matthew 6:22-23

In Winter, when the hours of light are rare and nights are long, we like the rest of nature, turn within. As we reflect on our inner being, we might ask ourselves: "What is the nature of light?"

To assist us in our understanding, let us light a candle and contemplate it. What profound mystery is concealed in a candle? Every time we light a candle, it is as if we bring a new life into existence. A closer look at the flame reveals two kinds of light: one which changes colours and another surrounding it with an aura of unchanging white light.

In Sweden, candle light is called "living light". The name "living light" suggests that life and light seem to have something in common.

Who is not attracted to the subtle light of a candle? There seems to be something in the candle light, which resonates with our own inner nature. We notice that a whole process of transformation is taking place. The grosser form of the body is gradually consumed and gives way to higher forms of fire and light. To manifest light, air is required, just as a newborn human being is said to be alive after having taken his first breath of air, which we call the first breath of life. In the German language, when a child is born one says, the child "perceived the light of life".

In the image of the candle flame, the analogy with man consisting also of 3 parts - body, soul, and spirit - comes to mind. Could it be that man's inner nature, when ignited by an inner fire of desire, will likewise transmute his gross body into the higher vibrations we perceive as light? In this context, we remember the initial spark with which the first light in the myth of creation came into existence, when God spoke: "Let there be LIGHT! But what is this LIGHT?

Let us listen once more to what Matthew had to say about light and understand what he meant with that mysterious image of the "single eye". "The eye is the light of the body. If therefore thine eye be single, thy whole body shall be full of light. If therefore the light that is in thee be darkness, how great is that darkness!"

We assume that he was well aware of the Sun's light, but obviously he considered sunlight as being only one part in the process of perceiving, and he expressed this by naming the other light "the light of the body", the inner light, as something essential in man. In his words, he tells us that we colour the world according to how receptive we are to this inner light. If we are able to receive it fully, if we are transparent to it, then it will radiate out fully and the world will be seen clearly.

To Plato, the light of the human eye and the Sun's light work in harmony. The German poet Johann Wolfgang von Goethe also expressed this thought with the following poem:

> Were the eye not of the sun,
> How could we behold the light?
> If God's light and ours were not as one,
> How could His work enchant our sight?

Here is the idea of the "single eye", the harmony between the outer and inner light expressing truth.

The fact that we play an active part in the way we perceive the outer world suggests that we should learn to understand the filters and glasses through which we colour the world. By changing our filters, our perception of the outer world changes. We effect the change insofar as our eyes become "single". Therefore we have to kindle the fire of our inner spiritual light, the light which brings meaning and love into the world. The spiritual inner light, the "light of the eye" as Plato called it, was a light of intentionality, a light that grants meaning to the world as we perceive it.

It is at the time of the winter solstice that Christians remember and celebrate the myth of the birth of the Christ. The light of the Son of God, as he is also named, has sent a signal of hope and a joyous message to mankind. Obviously man has recognized that in the mystery of the incarnation of Christ, something was achieved and revealed which is of universal significance and marks a turning point in the history of mankind. Why was this message so little understood and realized?

The reason might be that man still thinks in terms of separation. Instead of using Christ as a living ideal that has to be born within each one of ourselves, we have put it out on a pedestal and venerate it from the outside. Christ's mission was and is to show mankind the way to reach a higher level of consciousness: Christ-Consciousness. In him a higher ray of Cosmic_Light was conceived and manifested. It is this light of love which for more than two thousand years has not ceased to draw people into its field of radiation.

In most cultures, the name of God is the symbol of wholeness: oneness of all that is, omniscience, omnipotence. Each one of us is an individual piece of that divine whole. We reveal the whole when we let the light of love shine through us. Only the fire of love has the power to penetrate through the darkness of the human version of materialized spirit. To bring to light our particular piece of the whole, this is our task!

Let there be LIGHT. Let there be the LIGHT of LOVE! This is the transformational flame that will bring man back into harmony with the Cosmic Light.

Teilhard de Chardin often spoke of love as the inexhaustible source of energy, and he often likened its power to that of fire. The symbol of fire stands in his writings for the warmth and radiance of love and light, as well as for the fusion and transformation of the elements.

With a grateful attitude for the insights we have gained from our contemplation on the light of a candle, we extinguish this candle now. We feel replenished with a fresh release of that spiritual energy, that is the essence of life and light itself: LOVE.

ACKNOWLEDGEMENTS

Many are the beings, visible and invisible, who have inspired and encouraged me on this most difficult journey of self-knowledge and self-transcendence. I can't name them all but I wish to name a few fellow travellers I've met on the path who have been vital and most supportive to bring this book to completion.

In particular I would like to express my heartfelt gratitude to Duncan MacDonald whose fine editing ability allows the essays to read so smoothly.

And I feel a need to recognize the invaluable feedback, caring support and continuous encouragement of David Alexander, who had the faith in me to get this work published. Your contribution is most honoured, David.

Last but not least I wish to thank Joanne Ehrich who unselfishly shared her gifts as a graphics designer in caring for the details of this project.

For those not named here I thank you all from the bottom of my heart.

May this work serve to help people understand who they really are so that together we can transform the world into a new unity, the unity of love.

www.ingramcontent.com/pod-product-compliance
Lightning Source LLC
Chambersburg PA
CBHW061054090426
42742CB00002B/36

* 9 7 8 0 6 1 5 2 7 8 4 1 4 *